Giving God the Glory

Potter's Hand Publishing
books by Sheila Cragg

Devotional Bible Studies with
Scripture prayers:

A WOMAN'S WALK WITH GOD:
A Daily Guide for Prayer & Spiritual Growth

JOURNEY TOWARD HOLINESS:
A Daily Guide for Prayer & Godly Living

Novel

All the Secret Things

Available at Amazon.com
on Kindle & paperback

About Sheila Cragg

Sheila Cragg is an author, editor, and a former English (ESL) instructor at community colleges. She graduated with a Bachelor of Arts in American Culture and pursued a Master of Fine Arts in Creative Writing. She served as an Associate Book Editor for Focus on the Family Publishing. Her devotional Bible studies, *A Woman's Walk with God*, *A Woman's Journey Toward Holiness*, *A Woman's Pilgrimage of Faith*, and *Near to the Heart of God* were originally published by Crossway Books.

Her web site *Experiencing Christ* (http://womanswalk.com) offers free Bible studies, a year of Scripture prayers, and two of her devotional Bible studies as ebooks. *Experiencing Christ* draws visitors from around the world, including 50 countries from Argentina to Zambia.

Her articles have appeared in more than 20 periodicals, including *Reader's Digest*. She lives on the central coast of California with her husband Ron and has two sons and five grandchildren who live nearby.

Giving God the Glory

A 62-Day Scripture-Praise Journal

Compiled by

SHEILA CRAGG

Potter's Hand Publishing

Introduction

Praying Scripture is an effective means of seeking God's guidance, relief from our burdens, and the answers we need. Praising the Lord, however, lifts our heart and soul beyond our daily needs into the glorious presence of God. If you have struggled with depression as I do, then you know how much we need to be delivered from our despair. I wrote these Scripture praises during one of my lowest times. I am so quick to beg God's help and slow to praise the Lord and have a joyful heart.

When I need encouragement, I often recite this verse: "Do not be grieved, for the joy of the LORD is your strength" (Nehemiah 8:10).

I have come to realize that sorrow weakens us while giving God glory spiritually strengthens us. I wrote this book of praises to help me give thanks and glorify God. Now in these difficult times, join me in praising God through His Word and honoring Him as darkness falls and daylight dawns while we wait for Jesus Christ to return.

Write your praises and requests on the lines. I have included a starter sentence to help you respond to the prayer, offer your own praises, and give glory to God. Be sure to date each entry you make.

1

How Majestic Is His Name

O Lord, our Lord, how majestic is your name in all the earth! You have set your glory above the heavens." I will glory in Your holy name; my heart seeks You, Lord, and rejoices. I will sing to the glory of Your name; I will make Your praise glorious! "Who will not fear you, O Lord, and bring glory to your name? For you alone are holy. All nations will come and worship before you, for your righteous acts have been revealed." Blessed are You, King Jesus, who comes in the name of the Lord; peace in heaven, and glory in the highest!

(PS. 8:1 NOT PARAPHRASED; 1 CHRON. 16:10; PS. 66:2 PARAPHRASED; REV. 15:4 NOT PARAPHRASED; LUKE 19:38 KJV PARAPHRASED)

PRAISES AND PRAYER REQUESTS

I glory in your holy name for

_____

_____

_____

_____

_____

_____

_____

_____

2

~~·~·~

Give Thanks to the Lord

It is good to give thanks unto You, Lord, and to sing praises to Your name, O most High, to demonstrate Your loving kindness in the morning and Your faithfulness every night. For You make me glad by Your works; I will sing for joy because of the works of Your hands. Therefore, I will give thanks to You, O Lord, among the people, and I will sing praises to Your name. To You, O God, I give thanks, to You I give thanks; for Your name is near as Your wondrous works declare.

(Ps. 92:1-2, 4; 2 Sam. 22:50; Ps. 75:1, all kjv paraphrased)

PRAISES AND PRAYER REQUESTS

O God, I give thanks, to You for _____

_____

_____

_____

_____

_____

_____

_____

_____

_____

_____

3

Enter His Gates with Thanksgiving

Lord, with all the earth I make a joyful sound to You. I serve You with gladness! I come into Your presence with singing! I know, Lord, that You are God! It is You who made me, and I am yours. I belong to You; I am a sheep of Your pasture. I enter Your gates with thanksgiving and Your courts with praise! I give thanks to You and bless Your name! For You are good, and Your steadfast love endures forever, and Your faithfulness to all generations. Praise You, Lord. Praise You for Your mighty deeds; praise You for Your exceeding greatness!

(Ps. 100; 150:1A-2 RSV PARAPHRASED)

PRAISES AND REQUESTS

I enter Your gates with thanksgiving for

_____

_____

_____

_____

_____

_____

_____

4

~·✥·~

Sacrifice of Praise

Lord Jesus, I will sacrifice a thank offering to You and call on Your name. Through You I will offer a sacrifice of praise to God continually, that is, the fruit of my lips giving thanks to Your name. I will sacrifice a freewill offering to You, Lord; I will praise Your name, for it is good. For You have delivered me from all my troubles. I will offer the sacrifices of thanksgiving and rehearse Your deeds with shouts of joy and singing!

(Ps. 116:17; Heb. 13:15 kjv; Ps. 54:6-7a;
Ps. 107:22 amp, all paraphrased)

Praises and Prayer Requests

I sacrifice a thank offering to you, for You

_____

_____

_____

_____

_____

_____

_____

_____

_____

_____

_____

5

He Holds Our Soul in Life

    I will make a joyful noise unto You, O God, with all the earth: For all the earth will worship You, and will sing unto You; we will sing to Your name. Meditate on it. We will come to You, God, and see Your works: You are awesome and terrible in Your doing toward the children of men. You turned the sea into dry land: they went through the flood on foot: there did they rejoice in You. You rule by Your power for ever; Your eyes behold the nations: let not the rebellious exalt themselves. Meditate on it. Bless our God, you people, and make the voice of His praise to be heard: Which holds our soul in life, and suffers not our feet to be moved. Sing aloud unto God our strength: make a joyful noise unto the God of Jacob.

(PSALM 66:1, 4-9; Ps. 81:1, KJV)

PRAISES AND PRAYER REQUESTS

Lord God, I see your works in

_____

_____

_____

_____

_____

6

Come with Thanksgiving

"God, we thank you; we thank you because you are near. We tell about the miracles you do." "You make the grass for cattle and vegetables for the people. You make food grow from the earth." "All living things look to you for food, and you give it to them at the right time." You give food to every living creature. Your love continues forever. We give thanks to You, God of heaven. We come to You with thanksgiving. Praise You, Lord! Thank You, Lord, because You are good. Your love continues forever.

(Ps. 75:1; 104:14; 145:15 NCV NOT PARAPHRASED; Ps. 136:25-26a; 95:2a; 106:1 NCV PARAPHRASED)

PRAISES AND PRAYER REQUESTS

God, we thank you because

_____

_____

_____

_____

_____

_____

_____

_____

_____

7

My Heart Rejoices

How good it is for me to draw near to Your heart, O God, for I have put my trust in You that I may tell of all Your wonderful works. I will sing to You, Lord, because You have dealt bountifully with me. For great is Your loving mercy toward me. I have trusted in Your mercy; my heart rejoices in Your salvation. For Your lovingkindness is before my eyes, and I have walked in Your truth. I have not hid Your righteousness within my heart; I have declared Your faithfulness and Your salvation. I have not concealed Your lovingkindness and Your truth. I praise You, Lord. In the days ahead I will praise You, Lord, with my whole heart.

(Ps. 73:28; 13:6; 86:13a; 13:5; 26:3 40:10a;
111:1a, ALL KJV PARAPHRASED)

Praises and Prayer Requests

I draw near to Your heart, O God, for _____

_____

_____

_____

_____

_____

_____

Journal Notes

Journal Notes

8

Be Thankful

"Praise the Lord! Sing a new song to the Lord; sing His praise in the meeting of His people." "Let those who worship Him rejoice in His glory." I will worship You, Son of God, in the splendor of Your holiness; may all the earth tremble before You. I worship You with gladness and come before You with joyful songs. Since I am receiving a kingdom that cannot be shaken, I will be thankful, and so worship You, God, acceptably with reverence and awe.

(Ps. 149:1, 5A NCV NOT PARAPHRASED;
Ps. 96:9; 100:2; HEB. 12:28 PARAPHRASED)

PRAISES AND PRAYER REQUESTS

Praise You, Lord, for

9

Holy, Holy, Holy Is the Lord

"Holy, holy, holy is the Lord God Almighty, who was, and is, and is to come.'" Great are You, Lord, and most worthy of praise, in the city of my God, Your holy mountain. You are the Mighty One, O God, the Lord, who speaks and summons the earth from the rising of the sun to the place where it sets. Gracious are You, Lord, and righteous; yes, my God is merciful. My mouth will speak in praise of You, Lord. Let every creature praise Your holy name forever and ever.

(Rev. 4:8b not paraphrased; Ps. 48:1; 50:1; Ps. 116:5 kjv; Ps. 145:21 paraphrased)

Praises and Prayer Requests

I praise Your holy name for _____

_____

_____

_____

_____

_____

_____

_____

_____

_____

10

~·⁙·~

Praise the Lord!

"Praise the Lord! Praise God in His Temple; praise Him in His mighty heaven. Praise Him for His strength; praise Him for His greatness. Praise Him with trumpet blasts; praise Him with harps and lyres. Praise Him with tambourines and dancing; praise Him with stringed instruments and flutes. Praise Him with loud cymbals; praise Him with crashing cymbals. Let everything that breathes praise the Lord. Praise the Lord!"

(Ps. 150 NCV)

PRAISES AND PRAYER REQUESTS

Praise the Lord for _____

_____

_____

_____

_____

_____

_____

_____

_____

_____

_____

11

~·⁖·~

Clothed with Compassion

"Sing for joy, O heavens, and exult, O earth; break forth, O mountains, into singing! For the Lord has comforted His people, and will have compassion on His suffering ones." "Blessed be the Lord, for He has shown me His marvelous kindness!" "This is my comfort in my distress, that your promise gives me life." Therefore, O God, as Your chosen one, holy and dearly loved, I will clothe myself with compassion, kindness, humility, gentleness, and patience.

(ISA. 49:13 NRSV; PS. 31:21 NKJV; PS. 119:50 NRSV
NOT PARAPHRASED; COL. 3:12 PARAPHRASED)

PRAISES AND PRAYER REQUESTS

Blessed be the Lord for He has

12

~·:Ø·~

A Strong LORD

I will sing of Your mercies, O LORD, forever: with my mouth will I make known Your
faithfulness to all generations. For I have said,
Mercy will be built up for ever: Your faithfulness will You establish in the very heavens.
And the heavens will praise Your wonders, O
LORD: Your faithfulness also in the congregation
of the saints.

For who in the heaven can be compared to
You, LORD? Who among the sons of the mighty
can be likened to You, LORD? God is greatly to
be feared in the assembly of the saints, and to
be had in reverence of all them that are about
Him. O LORD God of hosts, who is a strong
LORD like You, or to Your faithfulness round
about You?

(PS. 89:1-2, 5-8 KJV; PARAPHRASED)

PRAISES AND PRAYER REQUESTS

O strong Lord, I will sing of your mercies

13

~~·ॐ·~~

No Other Name

You are the Lord. You have called me in righteousness. You have taken me by the hand and kept me; You were given as a covenant to the people, a light to the nations, to open the eyes that are blind, to bring out the prisoners from the dungeon and from the prison those who sit in darkness. "This is right and is acceptable in the sight of God our Savior, who desires everyone to be saved and to come to the knowledge of the truth." For "'There is salvation in no one else! There is no other name in all of heaven for people to call on to save them.'"

(ISA. 42:6-7 NRSV PARAPHRASED; 1 TIM. 2:3-4 NRSV;
ACTS 4:12 NLT NOT PARAPHRASED)

PRAISES AND PRAYER REQUESTS

Jesus, I believe there is salvation in no other name but Yours. I call on you to

_____

_____

_____

_____

_____

_____

_____

14

My Soul Thirsts for You

O God, you are my God; I earnestly search for you. My soul thirsts for you; my whole body longs for you in this parched and weary land where there is no water. I have seen you in your sanctuary and gazed upon your power and glory. Your unfailing love is better than life itself; how I praise you!

I will praise you as long as I live, lifting up my hands to you in prayer. You satisfy me more than the richest feast. I will praise you with songs of joy. I lie awake thinking of you, meditating on you through the night. Because you are my helper, I sing for joy in the shadow of your wings. I cling to you; your strong right hand holds me securely.

(PS. 63:1-8, NLT, NOT PARAPHRASED)

PRAISES AND PRAYER REQUESTS

Because you are my helper, I

_____

_____

_____

_____

_____

_____

Journal Notes

Journal Notes

15

The Voice of the LORD

Give unto the LORD, O you mighty, give unto the LORD glory and strength. Give unto the LORD the glory due unto his name; worship the LORD in the beauty of holiness. The voice of the LORD is upon the waters: the God of glory thunders: the LORD is upon many waters. The voice of the LORD is powerful; the voice of the LORD is full of majesty. The voice of the LORD breaks the cedars; yes, the LORD breaks the cedars of Lebanon. He makes them also to skip like a calf; Lebanon and Sirion like a young unicorn. The voice of the LORD divides the flames of fire. The voice of the LORD shakes the wilderness; the LORD shakes the wilderness of Kadesh. The voice of the LORD makes the hinds to calve, and discovers the forests: and in his temple everyone speaks of his glory. The LORD sits upon the flood; yes, the LORD sits King for ever. The LORD will give strength unto his people; the LORD will bless his people with peace.

(PS. 29 KJV, PARAPHRASED)

PRAISES AND PRAYER REQUESTS

O LORD give me strength to _____

_____

_____

16

❧

Find Joy in Gods Strength

I find joy in Your strength, O Lord, and in Your salvation I will greatly rejoice! You have given me my heart's desire and have not withheld what I requested. For You presented me with the blessings of goodness. I asked life of You, and You gave it to me, even length of days forever and ever. Your glory is great in Your salvation; honor and majesty You have laid upon me. For You have made me most blessed forever; You have made me exceedingly glad in Your presence. Be exalted, O Lord, in Your own strength; I will sing and praise Your greatness.

(Ps. 21:1-3a, 4-6, 13 kjv paraphrased)

Praises and Prayer Requests

O Lord, You have made me exceedingly glad because

_____

_____

_____

_____

_____

_____

_____

_____

_____

17

Tell the Wonders of God,

"The heavens keep telling the wonders of God, and the skies declare what he has done. Each day informs the following day; each night announces to the next. They don't speak a word, and there is never the sound of a voice. Yet their message reaches all the earth, and it travels around the world. In the heavens a tent is set up for the sun. It rises like a bridegroom and gets ready like a hero eager to run a race. It travels all the way across the sky. Nothing hides from its heat.

"The Law of the LORD is perfect; it gives us new life. His teachings last forever, and they give wisdom to ordinary people. The LORD'S instruction is right; it makes our hearts glad. His commands shine brightly, and they give us light. Worshiping the LORD is sacred; he will always be worshiped. All of his decisions are correct and fair."

(PSALM 19:1-9 CEV, NOT PARAPHRASED)

PRAISES AND PRAYER REQUESTS

LORD, *give me light through your Word that*

_____

_____

_____

18

~⋙⋘~

Faith of Great Worth

O Lord, "I am still not all I should be, but I am focusing all my energies on this one thing: Forgetting the past and looking forward to what lies ahead, I strain to reach the end of the race and receive the prize for which God, through Christ Jesus, is calling us up to heaven." In this I greatly rejoice, though now for a little while I may have had to suffer grief in all kinds of trials. These have come so that my faith—of greater worth than gold, which perishes even though refined by fire—may be proved genuine and may result in praise, glory, and honor when You are revealed, Jesus Christ my Lord.

(PHIL. 3:13-14 NLT NOT PARAPHRASED; 1 PETER 1:5-7 PARAPHRASED)

PRAISES AND PRAYER REQUESTS

O Lord, I am focusing all my energies on this one thing

_____

_____

_____

_____

_____

_____

_____

19

~·◊·~

Remember His Benefits

Bless the Lord, O my soul, and do not forget all His benefits, who forgives all my iniquity, who heals all my diseases, who redeems my life from destruction, who crowns me with lovingkindness and tender mercies, who satisfies me with good as long as I live. "Bless the Lord, O my soul: and all that is within me, bless His holy name."

(Ps. 103:2-3 NRSV; Ps. 103:4 NKJV; Ps. 103:5A NRSV
PARAPHRASED; Ps. 103:1 KJV NOT PARAPHRASED)

PRAISES AND PRAYER REQUESTS

Bless the Lord, O my soul for

_____

_____

_____

_____

_____

_____

_____

_____

_____

_____

_____

_____

20

His Wonderful Deeds

O Lord, "I remember the days of old. I ponder all your great works. I think about what you have done." "O Lord my God, you have done many miracles for us. Your plans for us are too numerous to list. If I tried to recite all your wonderful deeds, I would never come to the end of them."

(Ps. 143:5 NLT; Ps. 40:5 NLT)

PRAISES AND PRAYER REQUESTS

O Lord, I think about what you have done for

_____

_____

_____

_____

_____

_____

_____

_____

_____

_____

_____

_____

_____

_____

_____

21

~·:◊·~

Rejoice and Sing Praise

O sing unto the LORD a new song; for He has done marvelous things: His right hand, and His holy arm, has gotten Him the victory. The LORD has made known His salvation: His righteousness He has openly shown in the sight of the heathen. He has remembered His mercy and His truth toward the house of Israel: all the ends of the earth have seen the salvation of our God. Make a joyful noise unto the LORD, all the earth: make a loud noise, and rejoice, and sing praise.

(Ps. 98:1-4, KJV ALL PARAPHRASED.)

PRAISES AND PRAYER REQUESTS

O sing unto the LORD *a new song; for*

_____

_____

_____

_____

_____

_____

_____

_____

_____

_____

Journal Notes

Journal Notes

22

~ ⚶ ~

The Voice of a Psalm

Sing unto the LORD with the harp; with the harp, and the voice of a psalm. With trumpets and sound of cornet make a joyful noise before the LORD, the King. Let the sea roar, and the fullness thereof; the world, and they that dwell therein. Let the floods clap their hands: let the hills be joyful together. Before the LORD; for He comes to judge the earth: with righteousness will He judge the world, and the people with equity.

(Ps. 98:5-9, KJV ALL PARAPHRASED.)

PRAISES AND PRAYER REQUESTS

I will make a joyful noise before You, LORD, for

_____

_____

_____

_____

_____

_____

_____

_____

_____

_____

23

≈꙳≈

Knowledge of the Truth

Heavenly Father, I approach Your throne of grace with confidence so that I may receive mercy and find grace to help me in my time of need. I lift up before You my requests, prayers, intercessions, and thanksgiving for everyone— for kings, presidents, and all those in authority that we may live peaceful and quiet lives in all godliness and holiness. This is good and pleases You, God my Savior, for You want all people to be saved and to come to the knowledge of the truth. For this reason, I rejoice in You, Lord. I give thanks to You because of Your righteousness, and I sing praises to Your name, O Lord Most High.

(HEB. 4:16; 1 TIM. 2:1-4; PHIL. 3:1; PS. 7:17, ALL PARAPHRASED)

PRAISES AND PRAYER REQUESTS

I give thanks to You because of Your

_____

_____

_____

_____

_____

_____

_____

24

~·୬·~

Worship the Lamb of God

Yes, Jesus, one day I will be among the great multitude that no one can number, of all nations and kindreds and peoples and languages, before the throne and before You. Clothed with white robes and with palms in our hands, we will cry with a loud voice, Salvation to our God who sits upon the throne and to You, Jesus the Lamb. And all the angels will be standing around the throne and around the elders and the four living creatures. They will fall before the throne on their faces and worship You, O God, saying, Amen! Blessing and glory, wisdom and thanksgiving, honor and power and might be to our God forever and ever. Amen!

(REV. 7:9-12, ALL KJV PARAPHRASED)

PRAISES AND PRAYER REQUESTS

Blessing and glory be to our God for

_____

_____

_____

_____

_____

_____

_____

25

~◦~

Songs of Thanksgiving

I will sing to You, Lord; O saints of His, give thanks at the remembrance of His holiness. Surely the righteous will give thanks to Your name, O God; the upright will dwell in Your presence. We are Your people and the sheep of Your pasture; we will give thanks to You forever; we will show forth Your praise to all generations. We come into Your city with songs of thanksgiving and into Your courtyards with songs of praise. We thank You and praise Your name.

(Ps. 30:4 KJV; 140:13 KJV; 79:13 KJV;
100:4 NCV, ALL PARAPHRASED)

PRAISES AND PRAYER REQUESTS

We thank You and praise Your name for

_____

_____

_____

_____

_____

_____

_____

_____

_____

_____

26

His Wonderful Love

I sing to the Lord because He has taken care of me. Lord, remember your mercy and love that you have shown since long ago. Your love is wonderful. By your power you save those who trust you. I trust in your love. My heart is happy because you saved me. I put my trust in You and rejoice; I will forever shout for joy, because You defend me; I love Your name and will be joyful in You.

(Ps. 13:6; 25:6; 17:7a; 13:5 NCV NOT PARAPHRASED; Ps. 5:11 KJV PARAPHRASED)

PRAISES AND PRAYER REQUESTS

Lord, remember your mercy and love to

_____

_____

_____

_____

_____

_____

_____

_____

_____

_____

_____

27

Be Exalted, O God

O God, my heart is steadfast; I will sing and give praise, even with all my heart. I will praise You, O Lord, among the people, and I will sing praises to You among the nations. For Your mercy is great above the heavens, and Your truth reaches to the clouds. Be exalted, O God, above the heavens and Your glory above all the earth, that Your beloved may be delivered; save me with Your right hand and answer me. God, You have spoken in Your holiness; I will rejoice. I rejoice in You, Lord, yes, and give thanks at the remembrance of Your holiness.

(Ps. 108:1, 3-7a; 97:12, all kjv paraphrased)

Praises and Prayer Requests

Save me, Lord, with Your right hand and answer me

_____

_____

_____

_____

_____

_____

_____

_____

_____

28

~ ⁓

Sing to the Glory of His Name

I rejoiced with those who say to me, 'Let us go into the house of the Lord. I praise you, O Lord, with all my heart; I will tell of all your wonders. I will be glad and rejoice in you. I will sing praise to your name, O Most High. I sing to the glory of Your name; I offer You glory and praise. How awesome are Your deeds! Praise be to You, Lord God; let the sound of Your praises be heard.

(PS. 122:1; 9:1-2 NOT PARAPHRASED; PS. 66:2-3A, 8 PARAPHRASED)

PRAISES AND PRAYER REQUESTS

O Most High, I offer You glory and praise.

Journal Notes

Journal Notes

29

The Light of His Presence

Almighty Ruler of heaven and earth, You rule the mighty sea and calm the stormy waves. The skies and the earth belong to you. You made the world and everything in it. Your arm has great power. Your hand is strong; your right hand is lifted up. Your kingdom is built on what is right and fair. Love and truth are in all you do. O Lord, let me live in the light of Your presence. In Your name I rejoice and continually praise Your goodness. For You are my glorious strength.

(Ps. 89:9, 11, 13-14 NOT PARAPHRASED;
Ps. 89:15b-17a PARAPHRASED; ALL NCV)

PRAISES AND PRAYER REQUESTS

O Lord, let me live in

30

~∙∙~

Shout to God with Joy

Clap your hands, all you people. Shout to God with joy. The Lord Most High is wonderful. He is the great King over all the earth! He defeated nations for us and put them under our control. He chose the land we would inherit. God has risen with a shout of joy; the Lord has risen as the trumpets sounded.

Sing praises to God. Sing praises. Sing praises to our King. Sing praises. God is King of all the earth, so sing a song of praise to Him. God is King over the nations. God sits on His holy throne. The leaders of the nations meet with the people of the God of Abraham, because the leaders of the earth belong to God. He is supreme.

(Ps. 47:1-4a, 5-9 NCV)

PRAISES AND PRAYER REQUESTS

I sing praises to our King

31

Speak of His Righteousness

O Counselor and Holy Spirit, sent by the Father in Jesus name, teach me all things. For I am like a deaf person who cannot hear, like a mute who cannot open His mouth; I have become like a person who does not hear, whose mouth can offer no reply. O Lord, open my lips, and my mouth will declare your praise. Then I will not hide Your righteousness in my heart; I will speak of Your faithfulness and salvation. I will not conceal Your love and Your truth from the great assembly. My tongue will speak of your righteousness and of your praises all day long.

(JOHN 14:26A; PS. 38:13-14 PARAPHRASED; PS. 51:15 NOT PARAPHRASED; PS. 40:10 PARAPHRASED; PS. 35:28 NOT PARAPHRASED)

PRAISES AND PRAYER REQUESTS

O Lord, open my lips, and my mouth will declare your _____

_____

_____

_____

_____

_____

_____

32

~🝳~

Worship at God's Footstool

I will sing to You all my life, Lord; I will sing praise to You, my God, as long as I live. May my meditation be pleasing to You as I rejoice in You. I will constantly tell of all Your wonderful acts. I will glory in Your holy name; my heart seeks You and rejoices. I thank and praise you, O God of my fathers. I exalt You and worship at Your footstool; You are holy. I worship You, Lord, in the splendor of Your holiness. Praise be to Your name forever and ever, for wisdom and power are yours. Amen!

(Ps. 104:33-34, 105:2b, 3 paraphrased; Dan. 2:23a
not paraphrased; Ps. 99:5; 96:9a; Dan. 2:20 paraphrased)

PRAISES AND PRAYER REQUESTS

I exalt You and worship at Your _____

_____

_____

_____

_____

_____

_____

_____

_____

_____

33

Lord, Be exalted!

Lord, I will rejoice in You; I will be joyful in You, God my Savior. I will seek You and rejoice and be glad in You; I love Your salvation and will always say, Lord, be exalted! Surely You have granted me eternal blessings and made me glad with the joy of Your presence. You have made known to me the path of life; you will fill me with joy in your presence, with eternal pleasures at your right hand.

(HAB. 3:18; PS. 40:16; 21:6 PARAPHRASED; PS. 16:11 NOT PARAPHRASED)

PRAISES AND PRAYER REQUESTS

Lord, You have granted me eternal blessings and made me glad for _____

_____

_____

_____

_____

_____

_____

_____

_____

_____

_____

_____

34

⁓·⅋·⁓

God Is Powerful

Praise the Lord, God our Savior, who helps us every day. Our God is a God who saves us. God, order up your power; show the mighty power you have used for us before. Kingdoms of the earth, sing to God; sing praises to the Lord. Sing to the one who rides through the skies, which are from long ago. He speaks with a thundering voice. Announce that God is powerful. He rules over Israel, and His power is in the skies. God, you are wonderful in your Temple. The God of Israel gives His people strength and power. Praise God!

(Ps. 68:19-20a, 28, 32-35 NCV)

PRAISES AND PRAYER REQUESTS

Praise the Lord, God our Savior, who helps

_____

_____

_____

_____

_____

_____

_____

_____

_____

_____

35

Promises Fulfilled

Father God, I praise You for the "shoot" that came up from the stump of Jesse, that from His roots a Branch has borne much fruit. I thank You that the Spirit of the Lord rested on Him— the Spirit of wisdom and of understanding, the Spirit of counsel and of power, the Spirit of knowledge and of the fear of the Lord—and He delighted in the fear of the Lord. He did not judge by what He saw with His eyes or decide by what He heard with His ears; but with righteousness He judged the needy, with justice He gave decisions for the poor of the earth. Thank You for the star that came out of Jacob, the scepter that rose out of Israel. Praise God, for that "scepter will not depart from Judah, nor the ruler's staff from between His feet, until He comes to whom it belongs and the obedience of the nations is His."

(ISA. 9:1-2; 11:1-4A; NUM. 24:17B PARAPHRASED; GEN. 49:10 NOT PARAPHRASED)

PRAISES AND PRAYER REQUESTS

Father God, I praise You for

_____

_____

_____

_____

Journal Notes

Journal Notes

36

~·❧·~

Consider the Days of Old

Lord God, I have considered the days of old, the years of ancient times. I have heard with my ears, O God; our ancestors have told us what work You did in their days, in the times of old.

One generation praises Your works to another and declares Your mighty acts. For You are good to all, and Your tender mercies are over all Your works. You have been our dwelling place in all generations. Before the mountains were brought forth or You had formed the earth and the world, even from everlasting to everlasting, You are God.

(Ps. 77:5; 44:1; 145:4, 9; 90:1-2, ALL KJV PARAPHRASED)

PRAISES AND PRAYER REQUESTS

Lord, I declare Your mighty acts

_____

_____

_____

_____

_____

_____

_____

_____

37

All Nations Shall Serve Him

Yes, all kings will fall down before You, God; all nations will serve You. For You will deliver the needy when they cry—the poor also, and those that have no helper. Lord, You will spare the poor and needy and will save the souls of the needy. You will redeem their souls from deceit and violence, and precious will their blood be in Your sight.

O Lord, Your name will endure forever; Your name will be continued as long as the sun, and the people will be blessed in You; all nations will call You blessed. Praise be to You, Lord God, the God of Israel, who only does wondrous things. And blessed be Your glorious name forever; let the whole earth be filled with Your glory. Amen and Amen!

(Ps. 72:11-14, 17-19 KJV PARAPHRASED)

PRAISES AND PRAYER REQUESTS

Blessed be Your glorious name for _____

_____

_____

_____

_____

_____

38

~·⚬·~

Father to the Fatherless

Yes, "let the godly rejoice. Let them be glad in God's presence. Let them be filled with joy. Sing praises to God and to His name! Sing loud praises to Him who rides the clouds. His name is the Lord—rejoice in His presence! Father to the fatherless, defender of widows—this is God, whose dwelling is holy.

God places the lonely in families; He sets the prisoners free and gives them joy. But for rebels, there is only famine and distress." "The Lord announces victory, and throngs of women shout the happy news." "Praise the Lord; praise God our savior! For each day He carries us in His arms."

(Ps. 68:3-6, 11, 19 NLT, NOT PARAPHRASED)

PRAISES AND PRAYER REQUESTS

I will be glad and rejoice in your presence for

_____

_____

_____

_____

_____

_____

_____

39

~⬩~

The Name of the Lord

Praise the LORD. Praise, O servants of the LORD, praise the name of the LORD. Blessed be the name of the LORD from this time forth and for evermore. From the rising of the sun unto the going down of the same the LORD's name is to be praised. The LORD is high above all nations, and his glory above the heavens. Who is like unto the LORD our God, who dwells on high, Who humbles himself to behold the things that are in heaven, and in the earth!

(PSALM 113:1-4 KJV, PARAPHRASED)

PRAISES AND PRAYER REQUESTS

Blessed be the name of the LORD

_____

_____

_____

_____

_____

_____

_____

_____

_____

_____

_____

_____

40

Mother of Children

Ever merciful Savior, You raise up the poor out of the dust, and lift the needy out of the dunghill; That You may set Him with princes, even with the princes of his people. You make the barren woman to keep house, and to be a joyful mother of children. Praise the LORD. Let all those that put their trust in You rejoice: let them ever shout for joy, because You defend them: let them that love Your name be joyful in You.

(Ps. 113:7-9; Ps. 5:11, KJV ALL PARAPHRASED)

PRAISES AND PRAYER REQUESTS

I put my trust in You and rejoice

41

Sing Joyful Songs

Lord, I come and sing to You; I sing joyful songs to the rock of my salvation. I come before Your presence with thanksgiving and sing a joyful song to You with psalms. For, Lord, You are a great God and a great King above all gods. In Your hand are the deep places of the earth; the strength of the hills is Yours also. The sea is Yours, and You made it; and Your hands formed the dry land. Yes, Lord, I come to worship and bow down; I kneel before You, O Lord God, my maker.

(Ps. 95:1-6 kjv paraphrased)

PRAISES AND PRAYER REQUESTS

Lord, I come to worship and bow before you

_____

_____

_____

_____

_____

_____

_____

_____

_____

_____

42

~⁓•⦿•⁓~

The Lord Reigns

O Lord, You reign; let the earth rejoice;
let the multitude of islands be glad. Clouds
and darkness are round about You; righteousness and judgment are the habitation of Your
throne. Fire goes before You and burns up
Your enemies round about. Your lightning
lightens the world; the earth sees and trem-
bles. The hills melt like wax at Your presence,
Lord, at Your presence, Lord of the whole
earth. The heavens declare Your righteousness, and all the people see Your glory. Yes,
Lord, You will reign forever and ever.

(Ps. 97:1-6; Ex. 15:18, ALL KJV PARAPHRASED)

PRAISES AND PRAYER REQUESTS

O Lord, You reign

_____

_____

_____

_____

_____

_____

_____

_____

_____

Journal Notes

Journal Notes

43

Christ's Great Love

O Lord, I pray that from Your glorious,
unlimited resources You will give me mighty
inner strength through Your Holy Spirit. And
I pray that, Christ, You will be more and more
at home in my heart as I trust in You. May
my roots go down deep into the soil of Your
marvelous love. And may I have the power to
understand, as all God's people should, how
wide, how long, how high, and how deep
Your love really is. May I experience Your love,
Christ, though it is so great I will never fully
understand it. Then I will be filled with the
fullness of life and power that comes from You.
Now glory be to You, Lord! By Your mighty
power at work within me, You are able to ac-
complish infinitely more than I would ever
dare to ask or hope.

(EPH. 3:16-20 NLT PARAPHRASED)

PRAISES AND PRAYER REQUESTS

*O Lord, I pray that from Your glorious, unlimited
resources You will give me*

_____

_____

_____

_____

44

O How I Love Your Word!

God of grace, I will lift up my hands to Your commandments, which I have loved; and I will meditate on Your statutes. O how I love Your Word! It is my meditation all the day. My soul has kept Your testimonies, and I love them exceedingly. I love Your commandments above gold; yes, above fine gold. Consider how I love Your precepts, and preserve me, O Lord, according to Your lovingkindness.

(Ps. 119:48, 97, 167, 127, 159, ALL KJV PARAPHRASED)

PRAISES AND PRAYER REQUESTS

O how I love Your Word because

_____

_____

_____

_____

_____

_____

_____

_____

_____

_____

_____

_____

45

~~•~~

Honor and Majesty

O sing to the LORD a new song: sing to the LORD, all the earth. Sing to the LORD, bless His name; show His salvation from day to day. Declare His glory among unbelievers, His wonders among all people. For, LORD, You are great, and greatly to be praised: You are to be feared above all gods. For all the gods of the nations are idols: but the LORD made the heavens. Honor and majesty are before You: strength and beauty are in Your sanctuary. Give unto the LORD, O families of the world, give unto the LORD glory and strength.

(PSALM 96:1- 7, KJV, PARAPHRASED)

PRAISES AND PRAYER REQUESTS

Give unto the LORD glory and strength for _____

_____

_____

_____

_____

_____

_____

_____

_____

_____

46

∾∾⋅⋆⋅∾∾

Mary's prayer

"'Oh, how I praise the Lord. How I rejoice in God my Savior! . . . For He, the Mighty One, is holy, and He has done great things for me. His mercy goes on from generation to generation, to all who fear Him. His mighty arm does tremendous things! How He scatters the proud and haughty ones! He has taken princes from their thrones and exalted the lowly. He has satisfied the hungry with good things and sent the rich away with empty hands. And how He has helped His servant Israel! He has not forgotten His promise to be merciful.'"

(LUKE 1:46-54 NLT NOT PARAPHRASED)

PRAISES AND PRAYER REQUESTS

How I rejoice in God my Savior for

_____

_____

_____

_____

_____

_____

_____

_____

_____

_____

47

Immanuel

Lord, You gave a sign: A virgin will conceive and bear a son and will call His name Immanuel. For unto us a child is born; unto us a son is given. Yes, Jesus, the government is upon Your shoulders, and Your name is called Wonderful, Counselor, The mighty God, The everlasting Father, The Prince of Peace. Of the increase of Your government and peace there will be no end, upon the throne of David and upon Your kingdom, to order it and to establish it with judgment and with justice from henceforth even forever. Your zeal, O Lord of hosts, will perform this. Thanks be to God for His unspeakable gift.

(Isa. 7:14; 9:6-7; 2 Cor. 9:15, ALL KJV PARAPHRASED)

PRAISES AND PRAYER REQUESTS

Thanks be to You, God, for Your

48

The Lord Is King

"Praise the glory of the Lord's name. Bring an offering and come into His Temple court-yards. Worship the Lord because he is holy. Tremble before Him, everyone on earth. Tell the nations, 'The Lord is king.' The earth is set, and it cannot be moved. He will judge the people fairly. Let the skies rejoice and the earth be glad; let the sea and everything in it shout. Let the fields and everything in them rejoice. Then all the trees of the forest will sing for joy before the Lord, because He is coming. He is coming to judge the world; He will judge the world with fairness and the peoples with truth."

(Ps. 96:8-13 NCV; NOT PARAPHRASED)

PRAISES AND PRAYER REQUESTS

Praise the glory of the Lord's name for

_____

_____

_____

_____

_____

_____

_____

_____

49

Gracious and Merciful

"Praise the Lord! I will thank the Lord with all my heart as I meet with his godly people. How amazing are the deeds of the Lord! All who delight in Him should ponder them. Everything he does reveals his glory and majesty. His righteousness never fails. He causes us to remember his wonderful works. How gracious and merciful is our Lord! He gives food to those who fear Him; he always remembers his covenant. He has shown his great power to his people by giving them the lands of other nations."

(PSALM 111:1-6 NLT, NOT PARAPHRASED)

PRAISES AND PRAYER REQUESTS

Cause me to remember Your wonderful works, for

_____

_____

_____

_____

_____

_____

_____

_____

_____

Journal Notes

Journal Notes

50

~⁓﹩⁓~

True Wisdom

"All he does is just and good, and all his commandments are trustworthy. They are forever true, to be obeyed faithfully and with integrity. He has paid a full ransom for his people. He has guaranteed his covenant with them forever. What a holy, awe-inspiring name he has! Fear of the Lord is the foundation of true wisdom. All who obey his commandments will grow in wisdom. Praise Him forever!"

(PS. 111:7-10 NLT, NOT PARAPHRASED)

PRAISES AND PRAYER REQUESTS

What a holy, awe-inspiring name You have for

_____

_____

_____

_____

_____

_____

_____

_____

_____

_____

_____

_____

_____

51

~ ·≈· ~

Mighty Praise

"What mighty praise, O God, belongs to you in Zion. We will fulfill our vows to you, for you answer our prayers. All of us must come to you. Though we are overwhelmed by our sins, you forgive them all. What joy for those you choose to bring near, those who live in your holy courts. What festivities await us inside your holy Temple."

(Ps. 65:1-4, NLT NOT PARAPHRASED.)

PRAISES AND PRAYER REQUESTS

What mighty praise, O God, belongs to you in

_____

_____

_____

_____

_____

_____

_____

_____

_____

_____

_____

_____

_____

52

~·ᘔ·~

Stand in Awe of God's Wonders

Yes, Lord, "You faithfully answer our prayers with awesome deeds, O God our savior. You are the hope of everyone on earth, even those who sail on distant seas. You formed the mountains by your power and armed yourself with mighty strength. You quieted the raging oceans with their pounding waves and silenced the shouting of the nations. Those who live at the ends of the earth stand in awe of your wonders. From where the sun rises to where it sets, you inspire shouts of joy."

(Ps. 65:5-8, NLT NOT PARAPHRASED.)

PRAISES AND PRAYER REQUESTS

You faithfully answer our prayers with awesome deeds _____

_____

_____

_____

_____

_____

_____

_____

_____

_____

53

~·ᵛᵃ·~

A Bountiful Harvest

O our Creator God, "You take care of the earth and water it, making it rich and fertile. The river of God has plenty of water; it provides a bountiful harvest of grain, for you have ordered it so. You drench the plowed ground with rain, melting the clods and leveling the ridges. You soften the earth with showers and bless its abundant crops. You crown the year with a bountiful harvest; even the hard pathways overflow with abundance. The grasslands of the wilderness become a lush pasture, and the hillsides blossom with joy. The meadows are clothed with flocks of sheep, and the valleys are carpeted with grain. They all shout and sing for joy!"

(Ps. 65:9-13, NLT NOT PARAPHRASED.)

PRAISES AND PRAYER REQUESTS

Crown this year with

54

His Excellent Name

O Lord my Lord, how excellent is Your
name in all the earth, who has set Your glory
above the heavens! When I consider Your heavens, the work of Your fingers, the moon and the
stars, which You have ordained, what am I that
You are mindful of me, the child of my parents,
or that You visit me? For You have made me a
little lower than the angels and have crowned
me with glory and honor. You have made me
responsible for the works of Your hands; You
have put all things under my feet: All sheep
and oxen, yes, and the beasts of the field, the
birds of the air, and the fish of the sea, and
whatsoever passes through the paths of the
seas. O Lord my Lord, how excellent is Your
name in all the earth!

(Ps. 8:1, 3-9 KJV PARAPHRASED)

PRAISES AND PRAYER REQUESTS

I thank You, Lord with all my heart for

55

~ॐ~

Sing Joyfully

"Sing joyfully to the LORD, you righteous; it is fitting for the upright to praise Him. Praise the LORD with the harp; make music to Him on the ten-stringed lyre. Sing to Him a new song; play skillfully, and shout for joy. For the word of the LORD is right and true; he is faithful in all he does. The LORD loves righteousness and justice; the earth is full of his unfailing love."

(PSALM 33:1-5 TNIV, NOT PARAPHRASED)

PRAISES AND PRAYER REQUESTS

Lord, You are faithful in all You do

_____

_____

_____

_____

_____

_____

_____

_____

_____

_____

_____

_____

_____

56

<hr>

Revere the Lord

"By the word of the LORD the heavens were made, their starry host by the breath of his mouth. He gathers the waters of the sea into jars; he puts the deep into storehouses. Let all the earth fear the LORD; let all the people of the world revere Him. For he spoke, and it came to be; he commanded, and it stood firm." "Blessed are those whose help is the God of Jacob, whose hope is in the LORD their God. He is the Maker of heaven and earth, the sea, and everything in them—he remains faithful forever."

(Ps. 33:6-9 TNIV; Ps. 146:5-6 NIV, NOT PARAPHRASED)

PRAISES AND PRAYER REQUESTS

O Maker of Heaven and earth, _____

_____

_____

_____

_____

_____

_____

_____

_____

_____

_____

Journal Notes

Journal Notes

57

The Purposes of His Heart

"The LORD foils the plans of the nations; he thwarts the purposes of the peoples. But the plans of the LORD stand firm forever, the purposes of his heart through all generations. Blessed is the nation whose God is the LORD, the people he chose for his inheritance. From heaven the LORD looks down and sees all humankind; from his dwelling place he watches all who live on earth— he who forms the hearts of all, who considers everything they do." Therefore, "my soul will rejoice in the LORD and delight in his salvation."

(PS. 33:10-15; PS. 35:9 TNIV, NOT PARAPHRASED)

PRAISES AND PRAYER REQUESTS

My soul rejoices in You, LORD, for

_____

_____

_____

_____

_____

_____

_____

_____

_____

58

~·☙·~

His Unfailing Love

Almighty God, "No king is saved by the size of his army; no warrior escapes by his great strength. A horse is a vain hope for deliverance despite all its great strength it cannot save. But the eyes of the LORD are on those who fear Him, on those whose hope is in his unfailing love, to deliver them from death and keep them alive in famine.

We wait in hope for the LORD; he is our help and our shield. In Him our hearts rejoice, for we trust in his holy name. May your unfailing love be with us, LORD, even as we put our hope in you." "Praise be to the LORD forever! Amen and Amen."

(PS. 33:16-22; PSALM 89:52 TNIV, NOT PARAPHRASED)

PRAISES AND PRAYER REQUESTS

I wait in hope for You, LORD, for

_____

_____

_____

_____

_____

_____

_____

59

Christ Died for Me

Heavenly Father, You demonstrated Your own love to me in this: While I was still a sinner, Christ died for me. For, God, You so greatly loved and dearly prized me that You gave up Your only begotten Son, Jesus. I believe in, trust in, cling to, and rely on You, Jesus, so that I will not perish and be lost, but have eternal life. For, God, You did not send Your Son in order to reject and condemn me, but that I might find salvation and be made safe through Jesus my Savior. This is how I know what love is: Jesus Christ, You laid down Your life for me. And I ought to lay down my life for others. I will love others as You have loved me.

(ROM. 5:8; JOHN 3:16-17 AMP; 1 JOHN 3:16; JOHN 15:12B, ALL PARAPHRASED)

PRAISES AND PRAYER REQUESTS

I believe in, trust in, cling to, and rely on You, Jesus, so that I will not perish but have

_____

_____

_____

_____

_____

_____

60

Be Joyful!

Praise the LORD. I sing unto You, O LORD a new song, and Your praise in the congregation of saints. Let Israel rejoice in Him that made Him: let the children of Zion be joyful in their King. Let them praise His name in the dance: let them sing praises unto Him with the timbrel and harp. For the LORD takes pleasure in His people: he will beautify the meek with salvation. Let the saints be joyful in glory: let them sing aloud upon their beds. And my soul will be joyful in You, O LORD: it will rejoice in my salvation. My tongue will speak of Your righteousness and of Your praise all the day long.

(PS. 149:1-6; PS. 35:9, 28 KJV, PARAPHRASED)

PRAISES AND PRAYER REQUESTS

My soul will be joyful in You, O LORD, for

_____

_____

_____

_____

_____

_____

_____

_____

61

⌒◦⌒

His Counsel Stands Forever

Sovereign Lord, Your counsel stands forever, the purposes and thoughts of Your heart to all generations. But I cried to You, 'My God, who lives forever. . . . In ages past you laid the foundation of the earth, and the heavens are the work of your hands. Even they will perish, but you remain forever; they will wear out like old clothing. You will change them like a garment, and they will fade away. But you are always the same; your years never end.

The children of your people will live in security. Their childrens' children will thrive in your presence. Say, Amen! Blessing, and glory, and wisdom, and thanksgiving, and honor, and power, and might be to You, Almighty God, forever and ever. Amen!

(Ps. 33:11 KJV PARAPHRASED; Ps. 102:24a-28 NLT
NOT PARAPHRASED; REV. 7:12 KJV PARAPHRASED)

PRAISES AND PRAYER REQUESTS

Blessing, and glory, and thanksgiving be to You,

_____

_____

_____

_____

_____

62

~·⚘·~

New Heavens and New Earth

Ever-living Lord, You said, "Behold, I will create new heavens and a new earth. The former things will not be remembered, nor will they come to mind." "Past troubles will be forgotten and hidden from my eyes." I will surely forget my trouble, recalling it only as waters gone by. I will not call to mind the former things or ponder things of the past. O Lord, You will do something new; now it will spring forth.

(ISA. 65:17, 16B NOT PARAPHRASED; JOB 11:16;
ISA. 43:18-19A NAS95 PARAPHRASED)

PRAISES AND PRAYER REQUESTS

O Lord, do something new

Journal Notes

Journal Notes

Made in the USA
Middletown, DE
11 April 2023

28621334R00050